ALEXANDER THE GREAT

ALEXANDER THE GREAT

BY
ROBERT GREEN

A FIRST BOOK

FRANKLIN WATTS
A DIVISION OF GROLIER PUBLISHING
NEW YORK – LONDON – HONG KONG – SYDNEY
DANBURY, CONNECTICUT

For D.R. Green

Cover design by Robin Hoffmann
Cover photograph copyright ©: Scala/Art Resource, NY
(detail of mosaic: The Battle Isso).

Map by MacArt Design
Photographs copyright ©: Art Resource, NY: frontis, pp. 26 (both Scala), 21 (Erich Lessing), 35 (Giraudon), 50 (Alinari); The Bettmann Archive: pp. 8, 9, 11, 36; North Wind Picture Archives: pp. 13, 15, 23, 24, 28, 30, 32, 44, 52, 54; The Bridgeman Art Library: pp. 40, 47, 58; Hulton Deutsch Collection: p. 56.

Library of Congress Cataloging-in-Publication Data

Green, Robert.
Alexander the Great / by Robert Green.
p. cm. — (A First book)
Includes bibliographical references and index.
Summary: Describes the life, battle, campaigns, influence on the ancient world, and mythological status of the champion of the Greeks who marched his armies as far as India.
ISBN 0-531-20230-5 (lib. bdg.)—ISBN 0-531-15799-7 (pbk.)
1. Alexander, the Great, 356-323 B.C.—Juvenile literature. 2. Greece—History— Macedonian Expansion, 359-323 B.C.—Juvenile literature.
3. Generals—Greece—Bibliography—Juvenile literature. 4. Greece—Kings and rulers—Biography—Juvenile literature. [1. Alexander, the Great, 356-323 B.C. 2. Generals. 3. Kings, 359-323 B.C.] I. Title. II. Series
DF234.G685 1996
938'.07'092—dc20 *95-43208* CIP AC
[B]

CONTENTS

He would always have searched beyond for something unknown, and if there had been no other competition, he would have competed against himself.

—ARRIAN, ROMAN HISTORIAN

1

A NEW ACHILLES

In the early spring of 334 B.C., a fleet of Greek warships under the command of Alexander the Great neared the shores of Asia Minor, which we know today as modern Turkey. Alexander had already slaughtered a bull in honor of the Greek sea god, Poseidon, to ensure a safe crossing to Asia Minor. Now he dressed in a magnificent suit of armor and snatched up a long war spear. Upon landing, Alexander was the first man to leap off the ship. He drove his spear into the soil of Asia, to show his determination to win control over this land from the Persian Empire.

Alexander's act was in memory of the great Greek hero Achilles. Achilles was probably Alexander's favorite hero as a child. He had read about him in

the great epic poem called the *Iliad.* Alexander's mother had taught him that Achilles was his distant relation. Achilles had tried to capture the city of Troy in Asia Minor. Now Alexander, too, came as the champion of the Greeks, to defeat their ancient enemy, the Persian Empire, led by King Darius III. He did this, then marched his armies past the farthest stretches of the Persian Empire, all the way to India. There, he believed, he would find the end of the earth.

Philip II, king of Macedon and father of Alexander the Great; when Philip was murdered, Alexander became king and waged war against the Persians.

MACEDON AND GREECE

Who was this ambitious warrior who thought he could march his armies right to the end of the world? Alexander the Great was born in 356 B.C., the son of King Philip II of Macedon and one of his wives, Queen Olympias. Macedon is a highland region that lies to the north of Greece. Its eastern shores are lapped by the waves of the Aegean Sea. Macedon was different from the great city-states of Greece, such as Athens and Thebes. These city-states experimented with democracy. The highlanders of Macedon were ruled by King Philip II.

The Greeks of the city-states existed in a constant state of rivalry and war. An Athenian named Isocrates had attempted to stop the wars between the city-states by uniting them into an alliance called the

Hellenic League. Greece, thought Isocrates, would surely be a better place if the Greeks only fought against foreigners and not among themselves.

Even after the Hellenic League was formed, the quarrels among the Greeks lingered. Little by little, King Philip of Macedon began to involve himself in the disputes. Macedon was not Greece, but it had adopted much of the culture of the Greeks, including their language and religion. So it was not so strange that Philip should yearn for control of Greece. One by one, the city-states fell to Philip's feared Macedonian horsemen and soldiers, who fought fiercely with long spears called *sarissas*.

ALEXANDER AS A YOUTH

Alexander was still a boy while these events were happening. He lived in Pella, the capital of Macedon, and he grew up with the sons of important Macedonians and Greeks. They shared in Alexander's games and schooling and also learned with Alexander the art of war. Many of Alexander's early friends would become his lifelong allies, serving as generals and advisers on his campaigns.

Alexander was a headstrong boy from the beginning. He was very handsome and very proud. He had fair skin, and throughout his life he remained beardless. Alexander walked with confidence, his head

This head of Alexander the Great is based on the bust by the famous sculptor Lysippus. It is said that Alexander would not let anyone but Lysippus sculpt his likeness. An epigram on a portrait by Lysippus, which the ancient biographer Plutarch recorded, suggests why Alexander was shown this way:

The bronze looks heavenward still, as who should say:
"Thine, Zeus, the skies; the earth shall own my sway."

slightly tilted to the left and his eyes turned upward toward the sky, as if to see the gods looking down favorably upon him. After his death, his posture would become the model form of the hero. Greek, Roman, and Renaissance sculptors would chisel their statues into his likeness.

The Macedonians were famed for their knowledge of horses. One day Alexander and his father went to a horse fair, where Alexander found a beautiful and noble-looking beast. No one could tame the horse. It jumped and whinnied if anyone approached.

Alexander convinced his father to buy him this horse, for he had noticed that the horse was really just afraid of its own shadow. His father agreed. Then Alexander approached the horse, turned him toward the sun, and mounted. Much to the astonishment of everyone, he rode calmly away. This horse, named Bucephalus, would carry Alexander to war against the Persians. When Bucephalus died, Alexander named a city after him.

When Alexander was thirteen, King Philip invited the Athenian philosopher Aristotle to become Alexander's tutor. In a short time, Aristotle was convinced that Alexander would become the "chosen vessel" of the Greeks, the one to carry forth the glory of Greek culture. He spared no effort in teaching him Greek philosophy, history, and a reverence for all forms of knowledge. Surely Aristotle filled Alexander with the curiosity that later drove him farther and farther east in hopes of finding the end of the world. Aristotle also tried to teach Alexander moderation. He wrote for the young prince a treatise, or guide, to being a ruler. But moderation was one lesson Alexander never learned. He did everything with a deep passion.

Alexander listens patiently to an oration by the philosopher Aristotle. Aristotle's boundless curiosity undoubtedly affected Alexander deeply. Aristotle was a student of Plato and contributed greatly to the advancement of Western thought. He developed systems to classify different branches of science; this interest in order and classification influenced his approaches to history and philosophy as well.

INTO EXILE WITH OLYMPIAS

Another strong influence on Alexander was his mother, Olympias. Alexander's love of his mother drove them both into exile. By age nineteen he had already proven himself a worthy successor to Philip; he had ruled Macedon at sixteen while Philip traveled abroad. A few years later Philip chose a new wife, named Cleopatra, who was the daughter of Philip's general Attalus. Olympias became wildly jealous. Alexander, of course, sided with his mother. During the wedding feast, Attalus insulted Queen Olympias, and Alexander threw a cup of wine in his face. King Philip was furious with Alexander. The young prince and his mother fled the king's wrath by going into exile.

But events would draw Alexander swiftly back to Macedon. In 336 B.C., during a great festival, King Philip was assassinated by his own guards. Many suspected that the Persians were part of this treachery. Alexander took his father's place on the throne, becoming Alexander III, king of Macedon.

The new king, bred since birth for greatness, looked east toward the Persian Empire. The Greeks and Persians had fought for supremacy over the eastern Mediterranean for more than a century. The Greeks had established colonies on the coast of Asia Minor. This irritated the Persians, who considered Asia Minor to be theirs.

Assassins plunged their daggers into Philip II, king of Macedon, just as he was planning a military campaign against Persia. Alexander's position as heir had been in doubt during his exile, but he took the throne without opposition after his father's death. As soon as he began his rule, he ordered the executions of princes of Lyncestis, who allegedly planned the murder of Philip. Rumors also flew about possible involvement of the Persians in the murder, thus adding a personal motive for Alexander's campaign.

In 480 B.C., under the leadership of King Xerxes, the Persians had successfully invaded Greece. Greece continued to resist, however, until the Spartan navy defeated the Persians at sea and a nonaggression pact was signed. The effect of that long struggle against Persia was profound. The Greek city-states bonded together, and the common hatred of Persia helped solidify the Greek national identity.

By Alexander's time, the Greek colonies in Asia Minor were once again under Persian rule. Alexander decided to free the colonies and avenge the invasion of Greece by bringing war to Asia Minor, just as Achilles had done.

2

ISSUS AND THE ORACLE

Before Alexander could set out for the East, he needed peace in his own kingdom. Philip's death had thrown Greece into revolt. The Hellenic League was on the verge of collapse. The tribes to the north of Macedon, in the area known as the Balkans, were becoming a threat. Alexander found himself in the dangerous position of having enemies both to the north and to the south.

EARLY CONQUESTS

Alexander acted quickly. First he turned south to subdue the Greeks. He attacked the hilly area of Thessaly by cutting steps (still called Alexander's steps) into

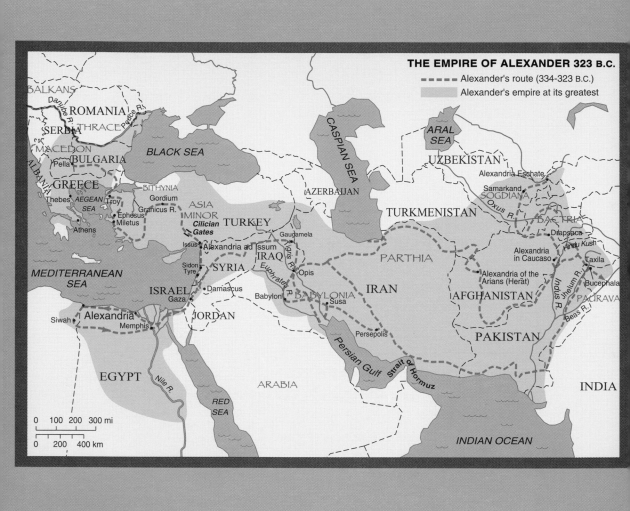

THE EMPIRE OF ALEXANDER 323 B.C.

- - - Alexander's route (334-323 B.C.)
Alexander's empire at its greatest

BALKANS

ROMANIA

SERBIA

Danube R.

Pedce R.

THRACE

MACEDON

BLACK SEA

BULGARIA

Pella

ALBANIA

GREECE

BITHYNIA

Thebes

AEGEAN SEA

Troy

Gordium

Granicus R.

ASIA MINOR

Ephesus

Miletus

Athens

Cilician Gates

TURKEY

Gaudamela

CASPIAN SEA

AZERBAIJAN

TURKMENISTAN

ARAL SEA

UZBEKISTAN

Alexandria Eschate

Samarkand

SOGDIANA

Oxus R.

BACTRIA

Drapsaca

Hindu Kush

MEDITERRANEAN SEA

Issus

Alexandria ad Issum

Sidon

Tyre

SYRIA

IRAQ

Tigris R.

Euphrates R.

Opis

PARTHIA

IRAN

Alexandria in Caucaso

Alexandria of the Arians (Herât)

Taxila

Jhelum R.

Indus R.

Bucephala

PAURAVA

Beas R.

ISRAEL

Gaza

Damascus

Babylon

BABYLONIA

Susa

Persepolis

AFGHANISTAN

PAKISTAN

JORDAN

Alexandria

Siwah

Memphis

EGYPT

Nile R.

ARABIA

Persian Gulf

Strait of Hormuz

INDIA

RED SEA

INDIAN OCEAN

0   100 200 300 mi

0   200   400 km

the side of Mount Ossa and swooping down upon the surprised tribes below. In Thessaly, Alexander captured horses, which he needed to increase the size of his cavalry. The horses proved to be a great advantage. With them, Alexander's cavalry swept quickly down upon the Greeks. He had little trouble defeating the city-states. Years of fighting among themselves had weakened them. The city-states surrendered with little resistance; the war in the south had come to a quick end.

The wild tribes to the north, however, fought savagely. One tribe, called the Triballi, fled to an island in the Danube River. With little hope of attacking the island, Alexander instead floated his army across the river. There he defeated the tribes on the far side. Once Alexander held both riverbanks, the Triballi were forced to surrender. Even the Celts, the northernmost people Alexander faced, pledged allegiance to Alexander. "We will keep faith unless the sky fall and crush us or the earth open and swallow us or the sea rise and overwhelm us," they said. They added that the only one of the three dangers they really feared was the sky falling.

While Alexander was away, rumor reached Greece that he had been killed in battle. Upon this news, the city-state of Thebes revolted. Again Alexander showed how swiftly he could move his army. Before the other city-states could join the rebellion, he attacked Thebes. He destroyed the city entirely, except for the temples of the gods and the house of the poet Pindar. Pindar, best known for his *Odes of Victory*, poems that praised winners of athletic games, had written kindly about the Macedonians. The fate of Thebes was reminder enough of Alexander's powers. All other city-states yielded without a fight.

It was in the spring of 334 B.C. that Alexander set out for Asia Minor. He brought with him more than thirty thousand soldiers and five thousand horses. His army was also accompanied by engineers, musicians, botanists, philosophers, poets, and actors, as well as siege equipment and a train of baggage animals that must have seemed endless.

Aristotle did not go east with Alexander, but he sent his nephew Callisthenes to write about Alexander's adventures. Poets entertained soldiers, but more importantly they noted events at each battle much as a news reporter does today. Their work helped make Alexander look like a hero, and they recorded his deeds for future generations. Callisthenes did this well when he was in Asia, but later when he criticized Alexander he was thrown in prison.

ACHILLES'S TOMB

Alexander's first stop in Asia was the city of Troy, the setting of the *Iliad*. This was the city where the hero

Homer's epic poem the Iliad *provided the Greeks with a heroic ideal. Poetry was the most sacred form of expression in ancient Greece, and poets were highly esteemed. Greek poetry was read aloud, so poets infused their verses with wonderful rhythms to keep the audience's attention. As a boy, Alexander always kept a copy of the* Iliad *under his pillow. He is shown here visiting the grave of Achilles, the hero of the* Iliad.

Achilles supposedly had perished. Alexander honored Achilles by dancing naked around Achilles's tomb. From the tomb, Alexander took a magnificent shield and a suit of armor.

Alexander was always concerned with pleasing the many Greek gods and goddesses. Before he left Troy, he sacrificed animals at the altar of the god Zeus and at the temple of the goddess Athena. Then he marched the Greek army south along the coast of Asia Minor.

In Asia, the Persian Empire ruled its far-flung lands through local governors, called *satraps*. Alexander had replaced the satrap of Troy with one of his own soldiers. One of his reasons for going to Asia was to liberate the many Greek colonies along the coast of Asia Minor from rule by Persians.

COMPANIONS VERSUS PERSIANS

The Persian leader, King Darius III, had begun to move his armies west to meet the Greeks, but he was still a long way off. It was the duty of the Persian satraps to join together and attack the Greeks even without Darius. At the Granicus River, the Greek and Persian armies clashed for the first time.

The Persians had chosen the site of the battle and had a stronger position. Alexander's general, Parmenion, advised him to be cautious. The Greeks

The Shield of Achilles, as described in the Iliad. *It shows everything from the constellations (the zodiacal signs near the middle) to scenes of everyday life in ancient Greece. Alexander claimed to be a descendant of Achilles. As such, he felt that he was not subject to the concerns of mortals, such as fear. The most essential proof of heroic character was prowess in battle, which Alexander showed throughout his life.*

would have to cross the river to attack, which would expose them to danger. Alexander dressed in beautiful armor and a shining helmet with white wings on it. Ignoring Parmenion, he arranged his armies and charged in the lead of his best cavalry unit, the Companions. Alexander led the Companions directly into the thick of the Persians and nearly lost his life. But the Persian lines broke under his charge, and the Persians were defeated.

After the battle at the Granicus River, Alexander seized the towns along the coast. This cut off the

Persian navy in the Mediterranean from any chance of resupply. The poorly-paid Persian seamen soon surrendered. Alexander had defeated their navy without ever going to sea.

Inland, in a palace at Gordium, the people showed Alexander a chariot tied with a very intricate knot of bark. According to legend, the man who untied the knot would rule Asia. Rather than puzzle over how to untie it, Alexander fulfilled the prophecy by cutting it with a swift stroke of his sword. That very night thunder and lightning filled the sky. The Greeks took this to mean that Zeus, the Greek god of the sky, was pleased.

Encouraged by this good omen, Alexander ventured back toward the coast through a mountain pass known as the Cilician Gates. As he moved east to meet Darius, Darius was moving west to meet him. At Issus,

The battle of Granicus, the first of three great battles Alexander won over the Persians

Alexander left his wounded soldiers behind and kept marching. The two armies marched right past each other without even realizing it, because they were on opposite sides of a mountain range. When Darius reached Issus, he slaughtered the wounded Greeks. When Alexander discovered this, he wheeled his armies around to face Darius.

FACING DARIUS

Issus was the battle for which Alexander had come to Asia. Darius himself was commanding the Persians. Darius probably had more foot soldiers, but they were not nearly as well trained as the Greeks. The Persian archers were more of a threat to the Greeks; Alexander kept his army out of their range until he decided to charge.

The Persians once again held the high ground. Alexander quickly sent his lancers to meet the advancing left flank of the Persian force, and he led the cavalry charge himself. The feared Persian archers fell before the charge. His double attack broke the Persian fighting spirit. Darius turned and fled. Without him, the Persian army had little hope of success. Darius had escaped from Issus, but he would not evade Alexander forever.

Even though King Darius had gotten away, he left behind his royal tent, chariot, bath, and other trea-

Ancient generals often personally led troops at the front of a charge. When Darius, shown here, fled the battle of Issus, the demoralized Persians suffered defeat.

sures. He also left his mother, wife, and two daughters. Upon seeing the luxury in which Darius lived, Alexander is reported to have said, "This, it would seem, is to be a king." Alexander treated Darius's family with the greatest consideration. Later, he married one of Darius's daughters.

CONQUESTS IN SYRIA

Alexander next decided to attack the Phoenician coastal cities of Syria. Phoenician seafarers had forged trade routes throughout the Mediterranean more than five hundred years before Alexander arrived there. The Phoenicians established trading posts along the Mediterranean coasts, the most famous of which was Carthage, founded about 814 B.C. near where the city of Tunis is today.

The Phoenicians remained independent of the Syrian capital at Damascus. Even after they were made a part of the Persian Empire under a treaty known as the *Pax Persica*, the Phoenicians were ruled by their own kings. They were the backbone of the Persian navy, however, with ships from the two ancient Phoenician ports of Sidon and Tyre.

Sidon welcomed Alexander, but Tyre resisted. Alexander began a siege that lasted seven months. Finally, Tyre fell. After Alexander defeated the city, his army slaughtered thousands as a warning to other cities in his path: Welcome Alexander or die!

Next, Alexander sent his general Parmenion east to capture the ancient city of Damascus, the capital of Syria. When Parmenion sacked Damascus, he used Syrian treasure to pay the wages of the Greek soldiers, and the surplus was used to buy supplies. Meanwhile, Alexander headed south, stopping at Gaza when he was wounded in battle, but then entering Egypt.

The Egyptians welcomed Alexander as their liberator and as pharaoh (ruler of Egypt). Alexander stopped at the delta of the Nile River, where that great life-giving river of Egypt empties into the Mediterranean Sea. He then marked the limits of a

new city with grain from his soldiers' food supplies. This city, called Alexandria, was to become the most splendid of all of Alexander's cities. After his death it would, for a time, be capital of Egypt and the most dazzling city of the ancient world.

THE ORACLE AT SIWAH

In the barren deserts of Libya came one of the most mysterious events in the history of Alexander. He visited the oasis of Siwah, which contained the oracle of Ammon, an Egyptian ram-headed god. This oracle was also associated with the Greek god Zeus, and rumor had it that Alexander might be the son of Zeus.

No one knows exactly what the oracle told Alexander at Siwah, but Alexander must have asked if his conquest of Persia would be victorious. Alexander seemed pleased with the outcome of the prophecy. He held a great feast in Egypt as celebration. Forever after, he called himself the son of Zeus-Ammon. Alexander was becoming a god in his own lifetime.

By sacking the Phoenician port city of Tyre, Alexander won his most difficult victory. He employed technical innovations in his sieges and demonstrated strict control of his forces in defeating a stubborn foe.

After visiting the oracle of Siwah in Egypt's Western Desert, Alexander believed himself to be the son of Zeus. This picture shows Alexander at an altar fire offering homage to the gods before the Battle of Gaugamela. Unlike his self-claimed ancestor Achilles, who offered human sacrifices to the gods, Alexander limited himself to animals.

3

THE LORD OF ASIA

After leaving Egypt, Alexander moved steadily eastward along ancient trade routes toward Mesopotamia. This land lies between the Tigris and Euphrates rivers in what is today the nation of Iraq. Alexander was once again on the trail of Darius and the Persian army.

Darius had already sent a letter to Alexander offering to surrender the western half of the Persian Empire. Since Alexander was occupying the western half of the Persian Empire, he replied that he would not bargain for what was already his. Alexander added in his letter that Darius should address him as the Lord of Asia.

Persian chariots fly through the Greek infantry lines. The scythes, or blades, jutting from the wheels cut down any soldier not fast enough to escape their furious onslaught. A line of Persian elephants approaches close behind.

FACING DARIUS AGAIN

Darius had little choice but to meet the Greeks in battle. He called up troops—archers, spearmen, cavalry, foot soldiers—from all over his empire. He added to this enormous army fifteen elephants and two hundred chariots. The chariots, wheeled carts drawn by horses, had long blades called scythes that could cut through infantry lines. Both elephants and chariots served much the same function that tanks serve in modern warfare. They were used to punch holes in well-ordered lines of infantry, creating an opening for attack. Elephants had the added advantage of upsetting horses that were unused to their presence and frightening soldiers with their size and strange appearance.

Again Darius chose the battlefield. It had to be flat, so that his chariots could run smoothly. The plain near the village of Gaugamela met the requirement. Darius held all the advantages. His army was larger. He had covered part of the plain with spikes and traps for the Greeks. He had smoothed other parts for his own chariots. When Alexander's army reached Gaugamela, an eerie calm lay over the plain. As usual, Parmenion advised caution. This time Alexander listened.

Alexander was well aware of the enemy's advantage in numbers. He made plans to use his own advantage—the skill and discipline of the Greeks. But Alexander would not, as Parmenion advised, attack the Persians at night. "Alexander," he said, "does not steal his victories."

Dressed in his magnificent armor, Alexander advanced to meet the Persians in the field on the morning of October 1, 331 B.C. Parmenion took the left. Alexander, at the head of the Companions, took the right. When the chariots attacked, the Greek ranks opened formations and the chariots passed harmlessly through. Darius's chariots had failed, but his soldiers were making some advances on the Greek left.

In the midst of the dust and confusion, Alexander caught sight of an opening in the Persian line. He charged through with the Companions, screaming the traditional Greek war cry, *alalalalai*. The attack brought Alexander within striking distance of Darius. Just as Alexander had heroically driven a spear into the land of Persia, he now hurled a war spear directly at Darius, king of the Persians.

The spear missed, but the charge was enough to send Darius into retreat. He fled, and the battle was over. At age twenty-five, Alexander had for the second time defeated the Persians in battle. Now he moved east into the very heart of the Persian Empire.

PURSUIT THROUGH PERSIA

Alexander hotly pursued Darius. When Alexander reached the ancient city of Babylon, its Persian commander Mazaeus surrendered. Alexander made him satrap of Babylon for wisely submitting. Darius, however, was still moving eastward, so the Greeks kept advancing. They entered the highlands of Persia through a mountain pass known as the Persian Gates.

Ruins of the Hundred Column Hall at Persepolis. The violence with which Alexander sacked the Persian capital may have been a result of the hatred that Greeks had long harbored for the Persians.

Then they moved toward the city of Persepolis, capital of Persia.

Alexander sacked Persepolis in grand manner. He burned the Palace of Xerxes to avenge the ancient Greek hatred for that dead king. He let his forces pillage the capital of their enemy. Its riches thrilled them. Never had they seen so much gold, so many jewels, and so many fine and beautiful treasures. Alexander now had the capital of Persia, but the king still eluded him.

It was now spring. Alexander left some troops

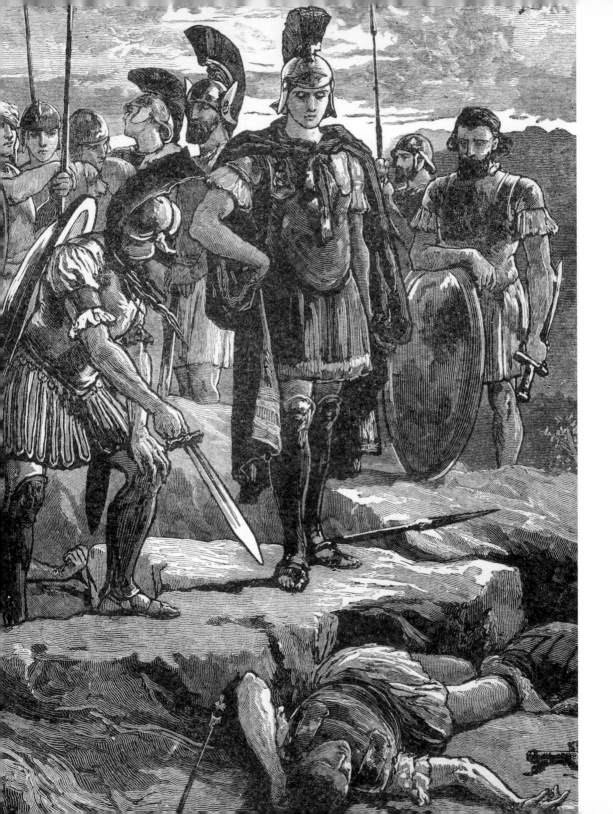

behind to occupy Persepolis, and he set out after Darius. He rode swiftly east and soon caught up with what was left of the Persian army. He learned that the Persians had grown tired of Darius's defeats and cowardice. General Bessus had led an uprising and taken Darius prisoner.

To avoid pursuit, Darius's captors had ridden into the desert, but Alexander was soon on their heels. There was no water to be found. The Greek troops suffered from thirst. Alexander shared their hardships, always setting an example, and they pressed on into the desert. When the Persian riders saw the Greeks coming, they thrust their knives into Darius. The Great King of the Persians was left to bleed to death in the desolate sands.

Alexander had respect for the dead, even those who were enemies. He covered Darius's corpse with a purple cloak and carried it back to Persepolis, the traditional burial place of the Persian kings. As a result of the murder of Darius, Alexander himself had become king of the Persians.

*Alexander discovering
the body of Darius*

4

INTO THE UNKNOWN

With the taking of Persepolis and the death of Darius, Alexander had fulfilled his ambition as the champion of the Greeks. Many of his soldiers now wanted to return to Greece to enjoy their fame and riches. But now that Alexander had conquered Persia, he intended to rule it. Furthermore, he still wondered what was to the east. Would he find the end of the world if he ventured still farther into the unknown?

The Greek soldiers had watched as Alexander adopted the god Ammon as a father at Siwah. He had also shed his Greek robes for Persian dress. He appointed many Persians as satraps instead of the Greek Companions. The Greeks grew uneasy as they watched Alexander adopt eastern customs. Some of the Greeks began to feel that he even preferred Persians to Greeks. They began to suspect that Alexander, leading them ever eastward, would never turn back to Greece.

TESTS OF LOYALTY

Soon Alexander adopted the practice of *proskynesis*. According to this practice, Greeks and Persians alike would have to bow in the presence of Alexander, as they would to an eastern king. Alexander commanded great respect from most of his men, but this was simply going too far. It was the Greeks, after all, who had introduced democracy to the Western world.

Not surprisingly, many of the Companions resisted. Some even laughed. Eventually, Alexander released the Greeks from this humiliation. However, he had already lost the support of some of his men. Soon a plot was uncovered. Philotas, general of the Companions and son of Parmenion, had been scheming against Alexander. He was put on trial in front of the army, condemned, and executed.

But the matter could not end yet. Even though Parmenion had served Alexander and his father, Philip, with distinction, he surely could not be trusted after the execution of his son. Alexander ordered that Parmenion also should be killed.

The execution of Parmenion was perhaps not as shocking in Alexander's time as it would be in our own. Alexander began to move east again without serious trouble from the Greeks. But their desire to return home continued to disturb him as he passed the farthest reaches of Persian civilization.

CLAIMING NEW TERRITORY

The new lands in which he found himself were not welcoming. The cities were very far apart. Alexander therefore dotted his path eastward with his own cities. He named every one of them Alexandria as he headed onward in search of Bessus.

Bessus, who had taken power from Darius, still commanded a troop of loyal Persian soldiers. Darius

Alexander's curiosity led him to discover the religious customs of the peoples he encountered in Asia. This page of an illustrated Persian manuscript shows Alexander before a Hindu idol. In India, Alexander befriended a Hindu wise man named Calanus, who traveled with Alexander's army. This meeting of Eastern and Western philosophy was retold in both Hindu and European literature.

had been Alexander's enemy. But he had been a king just as Alexander was. Alexander felt he had to punish Darius's murderers, because he respected royalty and therefore looked on the murder of Darius as treachery. More recently, Bessus had committed an even graver crime. He had begun to call himself Great King and to wear a crown in the manner of the Persian king. Alexander crossed through the rugged Hindu Kush into what is today Afghanistan. Then he chased Bessus north across the Oxus River into the kingdom of Sogdiana (roughly modern Uzbekistan).

The Sogdianan king, Spitamenes, at first welcomed Alexander into his kingdom. He allowed Alexander to catch Bessus and occupy the city of Samarkand. All was going according to plan. Bessus was sent into exile with his nose and ears cut off. Then, suddenly, Spitamenes and the tribes of Sogdiana revolted against Alexander. He found himself at war again.

The lands of Sogdiana were some of the roughest in the world, and Spitamenes was undoubtedly a great warrior. It was only through the treachery of a local tribe, tired of war, that he was defeated. The tribe assassinated Spitamenes and sent his head to Alexander.

Even though Spitamenes had revolted, Alexander respected him for his bravery and pride. To honor his dead foe, Alexander arranged a marriage between his companion Seleucus and Spitamenes's daughter, Apama. After Alexander's death, these two founded a dynasty in the lands of ancient Syria.

TRAGEDY IN SAMARKAND

The war in Sogdiana was not completely over yet, and at a feast in Alexander's encampment in the town of Samarkand something tragic happened. Alexander tended to sit up late with his companions, telling stories and drinking wine. Since he was an intelligent man and curious about the new lands he was exploring, he usually enjoyed talking much more than drinking.

But one night in Samarkand, Alexander drank too much wine. He got into an argument with Cleitus, a trusted general who had saved his life at the battle at the Granicus River. Cleitus was angry about proskynesis and the appointment of Persians as satraps.

Cleitus argued so vehemently that he caused Alexander to fly into a rage. Guards pulled Cleitus from the room before Alexander could do him any harm. But, unwisely, Cleitus made his way back into the banquet hall to continue the argument. Finally, Alexander seized a spear and drove it through Cleitus's breast.

The tragedy could not have weighed more heavi-

ly on Alexander, for he had acted unjustly in a fit of rage. This was not the mark of a great leader. He shut himself within his tent for three days, weeping and refusing to eat.

Finally, Alexander's soothsayers and advisers convinced him that Cleitus deserved his fate for neglecting the gods. And so Alexander began to eat again. After Alexander's death, a Roman historian kindly remarked that many kings had done evil, but he had never heard of another who repented.

Of the many characteristics that Alexander shared with his mythological ancestor Achilles, his furious temper was the most lamentable. After driving a spear through Cleitus in a fit of rage, Alexander fell into a deep spell of mourning. He was so upset that the morale of his troops began to fall; to counteract this, some of his companions spread a rumor that Cleitus had been a traitor.

5
DREAM'S END

With the wild northern lands of Sogdiana sub-dued, Alexander recruited a massive army for the invasion of India. India to Alexander was the land of the Indus River valley. He had been taught geography as a child by Aristotle and others, but they had little idea what lay beyond the Indus. Most of the land that Alexander called India is located in the modern country of Pakistan, but part of it is in the present-day country of India as well.

In the spring of 326 B.C. Alexander crossed the Indus River. He was welcomed into the city of Taxila by its *rajah*, or king, named Taxiles. Taxila had recently begun to fight against the neighboring kingdom of Paurava, led by King Porus, located in what is today

Topped with howdahs, *or turreted seats, which held the* mahouts, *or elephant drivers, and archers, King Porus's Indian elephants lumber into battle at the Jhelum River. The elephants posed a serious threat to the Greeks, but Alexander's foot soldiers hamstrung the giant beasts with axes and curved scimitars.*

the Indian state of Kashmir. The city of Taxila had long looked to the Persian Empire for protection from the tribes of India. Now Taxiles asked the new Great King, Alexander, to fight against Porus.

It was monsoon season in India at the time. During monsoons the sky opens and the rain pours for weeks and even months. To the Greeks, it must have appeared that the gods were angry. Nevertheless,

Alexander regrouped his armies, adding Indian archers and elephants to his troops. Then he went to meet Porus at the Jhelum River.

ALEXANDER VERSUS PORUS

Alexander's elephants were of little use, for they upset his horses, but Porus's elephants caused a bloody slaughter and much confusion. Alexander was greatly impressed by the Indians' skill at archery and their discipline. Many died on both sides. The battle was perhaps Alexander's toughest since Gaugamela. Porus looked magnificent in battle. He was strong and tall, and he rode an enormous Indian elephant. Alexander admired him greatly, as he admired all who fought courageously.

In the end, Alexander triumphed. Porus himself had been wounded by an arrow, and Alexander approached him on the battlefield. When Alexander asked in his noble way how Porus would like to be treated, Porus replied, "Like a king." And so he was. Alexander placed Porus back on his throne and enlarged his kingdom. Alexander could be very generous to his enemies—after he had defeated them!

By this time, Alexander had heard stories of the vast lands that lay beyond the Indus River valley. He realized that he was not at the world's end, but simply on the threshold of another part of the world. He hungered to venture into the mysterious lands of India. But his soldiers had had enough.

THE END OF THE LINE

In 325 B.C. at the Beas River, the Greek soldiers refused to follow Alexander any farther. With him they had seen wonders beyond belief and received vast riches, but they still wished to see Greece before they died and to enjoy a bit of fame and fortune.

This was Alexander's greatest defeat. His dream was coming to an end, because he could not go on without his army. He suffered bitterly. It made matters worse that Bucephalus, his faithful horse, had been struck dead in the battle against Porus. Alexander founded the city of Bucephala in honor of his horse. Then he returned with his army to the Jhelum River, where his carpenters had begun to construct a fleet of ships.

Alexander could not venture into India, but he could at least solve the puzzle of the geography of the waterways to the south of the Indus River system. These were called the Outer Ocean, but we know it today as the Indian Ocean. Alexander's ships traveled south on the river system under the command of Alexander's lifelong friend Nearchus the Cretan. Alexander himself marched the army along the river's shores.

Alexander and Bucephalus

The hardships of the journey to the Outer Ocean rivaled any they had suffered. Storms wrecked many of the ships in the rivers. Both the fleet and the army met heavy resistance from Indian tribes. In one battle, Alexander was hit in the chest by an arrow. He was saved by the shield of Achilles, which his shield bearer used to protect him until his soldiers could carry him to safety. Upon reaching the Outer Ocean, Nearchus and Alexander lost contact. While the army withered from heat and starvation, the navy sailed into the unknown waters of the Indian Ocean.

Alexander's army struggled through the desert lands of the Middle East. Upon reaching the Straits of Hormuz, where the Indian Ocean flows into the Persian Gulf, Alexander stopped and waited with a sad heart for Nearchus and the ships. He began to believe that he had sent his friend to his death. He was overjoyed when a search party found Nearchus, looking like an unkempt savage. Nearchus and his men had suffered greatly, but they had survived.

THE DEATH OF ALEXANDER

Once Alexander got back to the heart of Persia, he found his empire in shambles. Petty tyrants had replaced his satraps. Alexander faced the eternal problem of conquerors—how to hold on to what one has conquered.

*Crossing the desert of Baluchistan in 325 B.C. was the
closest Alexander ever came to destroying his own army.
The Greek soldiers suffered bitterly as the temperature
soared over one hundred degrees and the wind and sand
bit into any exposed skin on the soldiers' bodies.*

History has shown that people resist being ruled by foreigners and that time is the enemy of the tyrant. But Alexander, showing his greatness, had thought this problem through. He would simply mix the peoples of his empire. The blood of east and west would flow together. He would rule over a kingdom of mixed tribes and customs, in what the Greeks called *homonoia*, or brotherhood.

At the ancient city of Susa, Alexander arranged to marry one of the daughters of Darius to set an example for the Greeks and Persians. In a marvelous ceremony, eighty of his officers also married Persians, and many of the Greek soldiers also took Asian brides. Great celebrations took place. Greeks and Asians feasted together. But the old ideas of Greek superiority were not dead. The old Greek soldiers resented Alexander's kind treatment of the Persians.

To make matters worse, Alexander appealed to the League of Corinth in Greece for the right to be made into a god in Greece. The League of Corinth was the main political body of the alliance of Greek city-states. Alexander applied for deification to gain political leverage over the League. Although the distinction between men and gods was not as rigid in ancient Greece as in our times, the League did not grant anyone the status of a god. They were openly offended by Alexander's request and refused to grant his wish. Just as his father had done before him,

The wedding of Alexander and Statira (also known as Barsine), a daughter of Darius; to Alexander's right are Hephaestion and his bride Drypetis, another daughter of Darius. Hephaestion was Alexander's closest friend, cavalry commander, and chilarch, *or grand vizier. The two couples served as role models for the eighty officers who were given Persian wives. Another ten thousand soldiers who had eastern wives were given generous dowries.*

Alexander the Macedonian was offending the free Greek city-states. Many Greeks, even the freedom-loving Athenians, really did accept Alexander as a god and undisputed leader, and his will as law. But in the eyes of others he was still very human.

At Opis, the ancient Assyrian city north of Baghdad in modern Iraq, Alexander received harsh treatment from his own Greek Companions. Alexander had decided to dismiss many of the aging Greek soldiers and replace them with Persians. The army felt it had lost its leader and rebelled. Alexander threatened his men. Then he pleaded with them and finally shut himself within his tent. The soldiers thought about their many years of hardship and victory with Alexander.

Eventually the army softened. Alexander's Companions tearfully made their peace with him, and another great celebration followed. Greeks and Persians drank together from a great silver cup that had once belonged to King Darius. Plans were made for an exploration of the lands of Arabia with the ever-reliable Nearchus.

But as rapidly as he had sprung to power, carving the ancient world into his own realm, Alexander vanished. After floating in and out of fever—probably malaria caused by a mosquito bite—Alexander died on June 13, 323 B.C. in Babylon. He was only thirty-two years old.

Although it did not contain the remains of Alexander's body, The Alexander Sarcophagus, *found at Sidon in 1887, is a masterpiece of Greek sculpture dating from the fourth century* B.C. *It depicts Alexander charging into battle astride Bucephalus. The tomb of Alexander has never been found, but many believe it lies somewhere beneath the city of Alexandria, Egypt.*

ALEXANDER'S LEGACY

Without Alexander, his empire crumbled. Some of his generals founded dynasties of their own. But the dream of a peaceful empire, mingling the races of east and west, died with Alexander.

What had changed, however, was the general view of the world. Ideas traveled with trade goods along the routes that Alexander had forged. For hundreds of years after the death of Alexander, the East lingered under the spell of Greek culture. Most visibly, Greek influence could be seen in the architecture of government buildings, arenas, and religious temples that were built after Alexander's conquest. Europe was also opened to eastern influences. Scientific developments, philosophy, and other advances in learning flowed westward with the spices, silk, and art objects of the trade caravans.

Alexander himself was transformed from a real person into a mythological character. He became the hero of legends that began in Rome and then passed through northern Europe during the Middle Ages and Renaissance. Stories were made up about his conquest of female warriors of Greek mythology called Amazons, and his voyage under the ocean in a glass bubble called a "bathysphere." Some said he had flown to heaven in a chariot drawn by two gigantic birds. Although these legends became less believable as time went on, the glory of Alexander's conquests and his role in shaping history have lived on to today.

Illustrated medieval manuscript, showing Alexander descending into the sea in a bathysphere

TIMELINE

490 B.C. First Persian War begins; King Darius I sends Persian military force to Greece; Athenians defeat Persian force at Marathon

480 B.C. Second Persian War begins; Xerxes leads invasion of Greece; Persian navy defeated at Salamis

479 B.C. Persian army defeated at Plataca

356 B.C. Alexander born in Pella, the capital of Macedonia

343 B.C. Aristotle begins to tutor Alexander

340 B.C. Alexander serves as regent in Macedon while Philip II is in Byzantium

337 B.C. Alexander and Olympius go into exile after Philip's marriage to Cleopatra

336 B.C. Philip is assassinated, Alexander becomes king of Macedonia

334 B.C. Alexander and the Greek army cross into Asia Minor

333 B.C. Alexander defeats Darius III at Issus

332 B.C. Siege of Tyre, entry into Egypt, visit to oracle at Siwah, and founding of Alexandria

331 B.C. Battle at Gaugamela

330 B.C. Darius III is killed by his own officers

327 B.C. Alexander and the Greek army cross the Hindu Kush and Oxus River in pursuit of Bessus

326 B.C. Alexander and the Greek army cross Indus River, fight Porus at Jhelum River

325 B.C. Alexander's army refuses to continue east

323 B.C. Alexander dies at Babylon

FOR FURTHER READING

DePuy, Trevor Nevitt. *The Military Life of Alexander the Great of Macedon.* New York: Franklin Watts, 1969.

Krensky, Stephen. *Conqueror and Hero: The Search for Alexander.* Boston: Little, Brown and Company, 1981.

FOR ADVANCED READERS

Fox, Robin Lane. *Alexander the Great.* New York: Penguin Books, 1994.

Hamilton, J. R. *Alexander the Great.* Pittsburgh: University of Pittsburgh Press, 1974.

Keegan, John. *The Mask of Command.* New York: Penguin Books, 1988.

Renault, Mary. *The Nature of Alexander.* New York: Pantheon Books, 1979.

Tarn, W. W. *Alexander the Great.* Chicago: Ares, 1981. Reprint of 1948 edition.

INTERNET SITES

Home pages and directories will link you to a myriad of Web sites about the ancient Mediterranean and Asian worlds:

Exploring Ancient World Cultures (University of Evansville):
    http://cedar.evansville.edu/~wcweb/wc101/
ArchNet (University of Connecticut):
    http://spirit.lib.uconn.edu/archaeology.html
ROMARCH, a home page on archaeology in Italy and the Roman
    provinces:
    http://personal-www.umich.edu/~pfoss/ROMARCH.html
The Ancient World Web:
    http://atlantic.evsc.virginia.edu/julia/AncientWorld.html

One example of the many sites you can visit is the *International Museum of the Horse*, with an exhibit that includes Alexander the Great and his horse, Bucephalus. Address:
    http://www.horseworld.com/imh/kyhpl1a.html

INDEX

Page numbers in *italics* refer to illustrations

ABOUT THE AUTHOR

Robert Green is a freelance writer who lives in New York City. He holds a B.A. in English literature from Boston University and is the author of *"Vive la France": The French Resistance during World War II* (Franklin Watts). He has also written biographies of three other important figures of the ancient world: *Cleopatra, Herod the Great,* and *Tutankhamun.*